The Old Things

Diana Noonan

Gran's house was small. There was no room for all her old things.

Gran asked Tom if he would like her old things.

To: Tom
From: Gran

Dear Tom,
Would you like my record player? I had it when I was a girl. You can play songs on it.
Love,
Gran

To: Gran
From: Tom

Dear Gran,
I play songs on my MP3 player, but I would like your record player.
Thank you!
Love,
Tom

To: Tom
From: Gran

Dear Tom,
My old camera needs film to take a photo.
Would you like it?
Love,
Gran

To: Gran
From: Tom

Dear Gran,
Thank you, but I do not need your camera. I got this digital camera for my birthday! I can see photos on it.
Love,
Tom

To Tom
From Gran Send

Dear Tom,
Would you like my old typewriter? You can type letters on it.
Love,
Gran

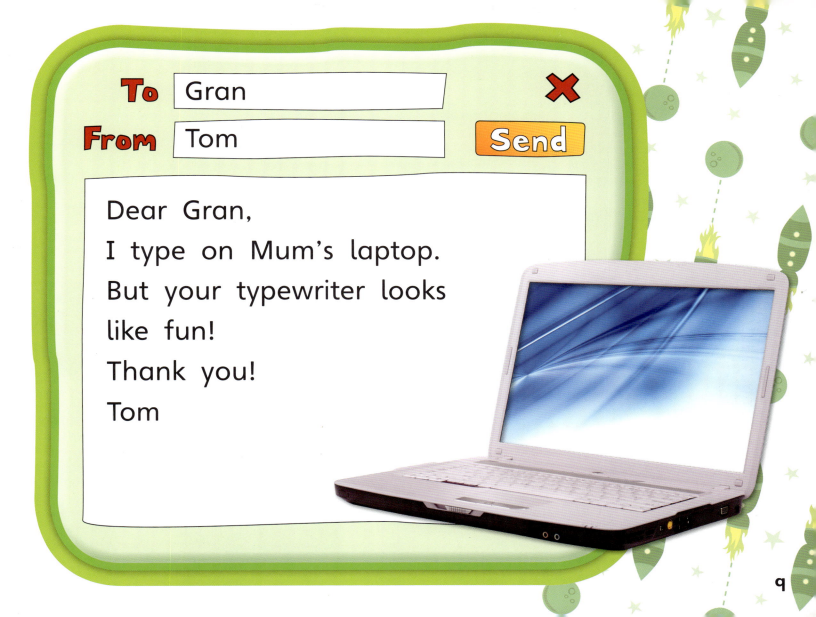

To: Gran
From: Tom

Dear Gran,
I type on Mum's laptop.
But your typewriter looks like fun!
Thank you!
Tom

To: Tom
From: Gran

Dear Tom,
Would you like my dad's old telephone? It is 90 years old!
Love,
Gran

To: Gran
From: Tom

Dear Gran,
Thank you, but I cannot use your old phone!
I can call you on Dad's mobile phone.
Love,
Tom

To: Tom
From: Gran

Dear Tom,
Would you like my old pen and ink pot?
Love,
Gran

To: Gran
From: Tom

Dear Gran,
Thank you for your pen and ink pot. I can use them with my pencils.
Love,
Tom

To: Tom
From: Gran

Dear Tom,
I am glad you would like some of my old things!
I will send them to you.
Love,
Gran

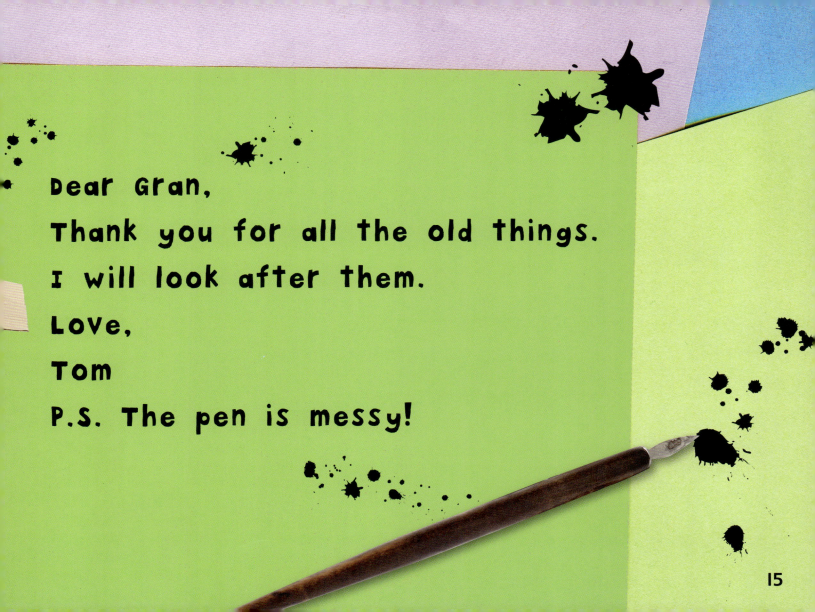

Dear Gran,
Thank you for all the old things.
I will look after them.
Love,
Tom
P.S. The pen is messy!

BACK THEN  TODAY

 record player   MP3 player

 camera   digital camera

typewriter   laptop

 telephone   mobile phone

 pen and ink   pencils